THE LIFE AND TIMES OF BRUCE SMITH

The Life and Times of Bruce Smith

VIETNAM AND BEYOND

Bruce K. Smith

AirMail Press Wivenhoe, England

To Vau

Contents

One

Foundations

Thinking back to Elementary School, I was already learning about competition and my surroundings with my classmates. Even when we were in class, everybody wanted to be the teacher's pet. Most of us were just regular, everyday people. There were a few rich kids, but most of us were regular kids with decent clothes, plenty of food, and a roof over our heads. Dad usually was the breadwinner, while mom stayed home cooking and cleaning. At recess, most of us wanted to be the best kickball player or get the best grade. I found out, to my surprise, that I was pretty clever at all of my school studies, so I tried to help other students who were struggling.

In the early 60s, the majority of people were Caucasian, with Spanish, Mexican, and a few Asians. There weren't many people yet in San Jose and no traffic jams. My dad never told us to be Catholic or Protestant, but that he wanted us to grow up and choose our own way. All he told me was whatever profession I decided to take, to be the best at it. He told me most people didn't like what they did for a living. He was in the war and fought in the Pacific on the Philippines Island. Even to the day he died, he never talked about it.

In my first year of high school, I took what people call the jock classes. I took radio, woodshop, and drafting. I wanted to see what I might like to do for a living. I took up basketball during my first couple of years because my older brother Eck was four years older than me. He was captain of the Varsity Team four years in a row. During my first couple of years, I met some guys who became my buddies. Most of them were tough guys and ran the streets because they were trying to fit in. All of us knew about cars and motorcycles. Many of them never went out for sports because of their financial situation. Most of us wore Levi's and white tee shirts or Pendleton jackets, and if you washed them too often, we got teased. That's where the term greasers came from. We called the wealthier kids the surfer boys because they had better clothes, houses, cars, and so forth. I chose the kids that were the street kids to hang around. We had our own code that made us family. We didn't rat on each other or anybody else. Although we were looked on as the bad boys in school, we were quite the opposite. Once in a while, we got a hold of some beer and kept to ourselves.

I used to kick it in the garage with my dad. That's where he taught me to use a slide rule and advanced math. My dad was a good man, but when he told you something one time, that was it. I borrowed his car one night and didn't gas it up. The next day, he went to work and ran out of gas. That's when he and I had our differences of opinion. I was his firstborn, so he let me run the way I did.

At least in our day, there were plenty of jobs for kids. Most of us cut apricots or plums. Back then, everybody had pocket change because the alley was full of orchards. Myself, I like cars. I mowed lawns, did yard work, tutored, and painted to make side money. I rarely had to look into my books to do my homework and would help others with homework and book reports to make some side money. My dad knew I could do anything for a living, but he was always upset that I chose to run with a bunch of wild ones. It never stopped me from hustling the way I did as a kid.

My dad was an engineer. He worked for Westing House and Lock-Keep Misses and Space as a draftsman. He would work outside in the garage, which he used to make all his drawings on the big wooden table. That's where he also showed me how to do calculus and trigonometry. In my Junior year in high school, I asked the teacher if

I could take a college entry-level math test. He gave me it to try and said he would return to grade it in one hour. When he returned, all he said to me was, "How do you know this stuff, and who taught you?" I obviously responded with, "my dad." So when class started, he gave me his stick and said, "Go ahead and see if you can teach these guys because you're one of them."

One of our best times in the '60s was going to the Fairgrounds. When we got there, we always ran into another gang. After one such encounter, we left the fair and chased them down the freeway. We were shooting at them with rifles and finally got them to pull over, but then the police showed up. There were about six cops, and when they searched my car, they found I had my dad's samurai sword and his M-I carbine that he had brought back from the Philippines. He took them off a Japanese soldier. After court, my dad had to file a pile of legal documents to get them back. No one pressed charges, and the judge gave us one year of probation.

Two

Running into Trouble

To us, the '60s were Happy Days. We had Mels, Spiveys, and all kinds of other hamburger joints for something to do. Most of the street kids hung out at Kings Drive-In. They could be found at Five Spot, Mel's, or Tiny's, if not at King's. The girls came out to our cars in roller skates and wearing hot pants. We just rolled down our window, playing our records for all of them to hear. We had 45 record players in our cars. We listened to Chuck Berry, Four Tops, Little Richard, and that good 'ol Rock & Roll. Before many Rock & Roll stars became famous, they played at our local bowling alley. At the bowling alley, which was called "The Bowlarium on Story Road," I saw the Righteous Brothers and Saint Dave there. The Everlee Brothers, Jack Diamond, and Tara the Snake Dancer also came to perform. Tara was always there. Tara brought along 14 snakes she wore around her neck while performing. Jack could play his guitar with his toes.

I think that King's had the most dangerous people hanging there. Most of the guys carried weapons you wouldn't really notice unless you carried them, too. The regular people who came in there to eat were never bothered by us, so we left them alone. The owner was a kindly woman named Anita, who made us promise not to harm or cause chaos in her place, and we did just that. The police were always stopping by for their coffee and donuts. Plus, if they were looking for someone, they knew one of us could locate them in a flash. In the back of the restaurant was a big parking lot where we had our Destruction Derby with any old junker cars we could find. As long as we cleaned up our mess, Anita was okay with it. She always watched our backs from the cops. She knew we couldn't get into too much trouble if we were in her place.

Once in a while, we jumped fences at the local wrecking yards to get parts off the junk cars. Some weekends, we would go down to Mexico to get our '55, '56, and other car's upholstery redone. One of my friends had an old '52 Ford with side lights, like the old police cars, so we painted the glass red and went up to Alum Rock Park to mess with all the lovers making out. We would turn on the lights to scare them into thinking we were the cops. One guy chased us and, on the way, lost control of his car and went over the cliff. We stopped to make sure they were okay. Then we took off like hell.

The local bar was called The Monkey Bar, and girls would swing inside the bar wearing only bikinis. I bought a phony ID from one of my friends and was forthwith caught by the cops. They told me there were several warrants for arrest for robbery and rape. I told them the guy I bought it from was a friend and who he was to avoid going to jail. I usually don't rat out a friend, but I couldn't hold it back this time. This time was different. One of my friends saw me outside with the police and gave me the sign. Shortly after, as J was alone, he pulled up in his Chevy with the windows down, and I immediately jumped in to get away. Sooner or later, the cops came to my house to see me again, and the judge suspended my sentence when I told him the truth.

One of my friends was a guy named Armond Blecher. Once, as we left a topless bar called Brass Rail, a guy who wasn't very fond of Armond threw his chain at him and almost took his arm out. Armond was a crazy guy. He picked up his bike and threw it at the guy, nearly hitting him. Armond was naturally nice, but you didn't want to mess with him. We were in a regular bar one night, and I remember a guy was playing a song over and over. Armond got so fed up that he walked up to him, threw him in the jukebox, and said, "Since you like this song so much, go ahead and listen to it now."

Three

The Catalyst

When I was 18 years old, I bought my first proper car, a 1957 Ford Fairline 500. My dad initially thought I stole it. Soon afterward, I was stopped by a cop who took one look at me and knew something was up. He asked, "Where is your license? Does this car belong to you?". I told him it was mine and I had paid cash for it. Then, I admitted to him that I did not have a license. The officer looked at me funny and then said, "Get in the car and go park in your driveway." He did not write me a ticket, but he did tell me to leave the car there until I got my permit. So I did.

During senior year, we were driving around, and my friends wanted to stop at a parts store. I saw them running across the street, dropping all kinds of boxes. I told them, "Please tell me you guys didn't just rob the store," as we took off. One week later, they arrested all of us. I was 17 years old and going away for grand theft.

The judge came out and said we were all going to get three to five years for armed robbery. Then he got to me. He said, "Bruce, some of these kids come from foster homes, drugs, and just bad families, but you come from a good home. You have no business in my court but an accessory after the fact; you're just as guilty under the law." Then, the judge gave us all a choice because the Vietnam War was going on. He told each of us it was up to us to choose whether or not to enlist, but should anyone choose not to go and end up back in his court, that would definitely be in serious trouble. He promised us that if anybody gets discharged with an honorable discharge, to come by to see him and he would clear our records.

As soon as the judge let us go, my father took me down to the local recruiter on Stevens Creek and said, "He's all yours!" Three days later, I reported to Fort Ord, California, on December 22, 1965, for military basic training. Following graduation, I was due to take surveying school and report to my first base in Germany.

Four

Boot Camp

When I got to Fort Ord, the Military Police asked why I joined before Christmas when so many recruits were on leave already. I told the Sergeant I was just happy to be there. My first days at Ford Ord were normal for new recruits. Hair shaved off, the issuing of all our clothing and supplies. I was assigned to C.3.3. barracks, about 10 miles from the rifle range. It seemed to me that most of my platoon were guys like me, high school dropouts, or just small trouble criminal records like me who were able to enlist with the hope of a fresh start.

Our barracks had four toilets and four urinals, and we were only able to use one or the other. We had to keep everything spotless. The floors, our gear, rifles, shoes, belt buckles, and I mean everything in case we had an inspection. We all paid the price if they found one of us that was not perfect. Sometimes, we had to go outside, hold our foot lockers over our heads, do the duck walk, and quack like a duck. Before we really started training, we all got our handbooks on the military code of justice.

We were woken up at 4:00 AM every morning and lined up in formation. Before going to chow, you had to go through the monkey bars. If you fell off, you had to go back to the end of the line. Our Sergeant was a Korean War Veteran with a metal plate in his head. He was one tough S.O.B. Most of our drill instructors were World War

9

II veterans. They taught us hand-to-hand combat, how to kill people with our bare hands, and never to panic. We also learned how to escape if only we were taken prisoner. They said our only chance was in the first hour before they could get organized. Sometimes, when we were fooling around, they reminded us that they were there to do the job. "Fine, if we didn't pay attention, you'd be coming home in a bag."

Every day, we had drills on marching in formation and how to march as a platoon. Everything we did was always as a unit. We had rifle training. Running to the rifle range was ten miles. You had to be in shape because you had to carry full backpacks, including your rifle, canteen, and so forth. They didn't like left-handed shooters because our rifles were M-14s and the positioning of the bolt. We were also trained on live fire exercises, which involved crawling under barbed wire while machine guns were firing over our heads as we crawled under the wire. We also had training, which included them using tear gas and CS gas. They took us into a building, and as we were going through the building, they threw the gas and took off our gas masks so we would know what it felt like. Tear gas just burned your eyes, but the CS gas made you want to throw up. They also taught us about nerve gas, which would kill you in a matter of a few seconds. You had ten seconds to put your rifle on one of your boots while putting on your gas mask.

Before you could graduate, you had to pass the physical training test, shooting a rifle while wearing all your field gear, and you had less than two minutes to complete the test. We were using the M-14 Rifle, which held clips of 20 rounds inside each clip. I sat down and kicked one leg up to rest my rifle on. The drill sergeant didn't like that very much, but my platoon sergeant told him to let me shoot my way. The challenge was to hit 100 pop-up targets that only stayed up for three seconds. Most targets were from 5 to 300 meters. I missed one shot out of 100 targets, which meant I won the trophy for Best Shot in the Company. This award was presented to me by Colonel Dielman.

The winners of all five events were supposed to get money and a three-day pass. Sadly, we didn't get three days pass because meningitis was found on the base. After graduation, we were all awarded two weeks' leave before we were sent to A.I.T., the second part of training.

Five

Learning to Survey

Off I went to Fort Sill, Oklahoma, to become a Surveyor. In the Army, surveyors were usually assigned to artillery units. Our job was to survey a spot every three or four hundred meters so that the artillery pieces could set their guns in the correct coordinates so they would be right on target when they shot the projectors. I never thought I would pass the class because surveying was all mathematics-based. The Sergeant said not to worry as we were all going to pass because there weren't any distractions to bother us. And as for what distractions there could be? Girls were the number one welcome distraction for fellows like me.

When I joined up, no girls were allowed in the military except for nurses and hospital workers, so he did have a point. We spent about half the time doing classroom studies. The other half, we were outside and in the field. We learned how to use the survey equipment. We used an attoliter to measure distance. We had steel tapes and markers. We used the tape, which reached about 30 meters, and put a marker in the ground. That allowed the attoliter machine to measure our distance, and we marked the spot with pins. While in the field one day, we came upon a giant rattlesnake. The snake was going down a hole when one of our classmates grabbed it and tried to pull it out. Naturally, he lived in the area and was used to encountering them.

In the second phase of training, we were allowed some time off during the day, and at night, we were allowed to go to the club and have a beer or two. Occasionally, they would give us a weekend pass. Naturally, we went downtown looking for beer and girls. After about eight weeks of training, we graduated and became Surveyors. We got ten days off before going to our assigned duty station, so I went back home to San Jose. While home, I went to visit some of my school buddies. I never really had any steady girlfriends. I was usually like a lone wolf. It seemed like I didn't want anybody else to be in trouble when I got in trouble.

My first assignment was to Germany at a place called Merrill Barracks, which was Hitler's SS Headquarters. When I arrived in Germany, there was a truck there to pick us up and get us to our barracks. We did most of our training up in the mountains called Artillery Post Number 3. They had old buildings and tanks there. We would call in artillery batteries to fire so we could hit those objects. If you were too far left or right or too short or too long, we could adjust our calls to bring the explosions right on top of the targets.

Back at the base, we usually got the weekends off. On my first pass, I met some wild ladies and woke up in a random hotel. By the time I got back to the base, I was two hours late, so after formation, the Sergeant told me to report to the commanding officer. He asked me why I was late and told me he believed me or would have written me up as AWOL. Then he said you're dismissed, and don't do it again. We had loan sharks there. If you borrowed $50, you had to pay back $100. On payday, they were right outside the barracks to get their money. After a couple of months there, I got bored. Eventually, I went to the commanding officer and told him I wanted a transfer. He reminded me that I signed up to spend my whole tour of duty in Germany. The only place he could send me was Vietnam. "Okay," I told him, and before I knew it, I was on a plane back to the States for two weeks of leave before I was sent to Vietnam.

Six

Into the Fire

The first time we went to Vietnam, we flew on TWA Airplanes and landed at Ben Hau Airport. Most of the 1st Infantry was in the Iron Triangle. This is where they dropped most of Agent Orange to kill the foliage in the jungle. We didn't have bottled water back then. We had water buffaloes and lister bags to hold the water. Anytime we drank river water, we had to throw pills inside and boil it for at least 2 minutes.

When I finally got to Vietnam, I was assigned to the 8th of the 6th artillery unit as a Survey Specialist. During my first duty station in Vietnam, I was assigned to the 8th of 6th artillery battery of the First Infantry Division. Our jobs were to survey in the artillery pieces for fire support for any units going out in the field. Most divisions were made up of about 10,000 troops. Some examples of our unit were the 8th of the 6th, the 4th Cav, which comprised M48 and M60 tanks, M113 armored personnel carriers, flame thrower 113, and the long-range reconnaissance patrol. The long-range reconnaissance patrol had their own Hueys and gunships. There were other artillery units and many Infantry Divisions like the 16th and 18th + 26 Infantry Divisions and others that I can't remember. So, when we left our base camp, which was in a town called Phu Loi, we had a starting azimuth, and from there, wherever we went, we took readings about every

300 meters. Our jobs were to know exactly where we were. We left markers in the ground so that the guys could park RT over our markers. The headquarters officer usually asked for a three-person team to proceed past our current position to recon the area.

I always volunteered to go because I got bored, plus I didn't come here to be another regular soldier. A three-person team consists of one person carrying the M60 machine gun and the other two covering their own weapons. We also carried our radio so we could contact the base camp. Plenty of times, we came upon the enemy's position, then we would call back for support. Usually, the 4th Cav would come up to engage the enemy. Sometimes they caught them napping, and sometimes they were too late. After we were done in the field, we returned back to base camp. While we were standing down, our jobs included filling up all the lister bags, checking all the outside latrine areas, and miscellaneous other tasks. About three months after that, I was itching for some action. The 4th Cav would send people over to our tent looking for volunteers. Every time the 4th CAV guys came around hunting for volunteers, it seemed like everyone around me just disappeared. I decided to ask 1SG Ryan why everybody kept disappearing. He told me grimly that if you went with the 4th Cav guys, you now had a 60% chance of NOT going home alive. The way the math worked out left only a 40% chance of survival with those guys.

The 4th Cav was a mechanized infantry outfit. They were always called on like Foremen's on duty. Hey, I've said it before. I am a little crazy. So, I volunteered to go with the 4th CAV as a forward observer. I managed to get the transfer approved by my higher leadership, and 4th Cav was where I was assigned for the rest of my time in Vietnam. After doing our job, we helped anybody unload shells for artillery units or make sandbags to secure our supplies.

When we were out in the field, I knew where all the Mormons were because they didn't smoke. Every day we got an S.P pack for 100 soldiers. There were 10 cartons of cigarettes and other supplies for everybody. We had c-rations for our food when we were in the jungle. We also had our cooks and mess trucks with us all the time. So

I would trade the Mormons some of my C-rations for their cigarettes. We had spaghetti and meatballs, chopped eggs with ham, peanut butter with jelly, beans and some fruits. Everything was in little green cans, and some of the stuff was from the Korean War. Everything to me was pretty good. I didn't have much to complain about. So when the mess trucks made S.O.S every morning, we called it "shit on a shingle," which I liked. It was basically chopped beef with gravy.

Seven

Cedar Falls

Our first mission was called Cedar Falls, a full-out mission of finding and engaging the enemy. It was sometime in August or September when we left base. We usually headed for Củ Chi, where the Viet Long usually were. It was usually known as Tunnel Ville by North Vietnam regulars. Some of the tunnels went down 10 or 20 feet, and then you ended up in a space about 30 by 50 feet, just like a king-size bedroom. Sometimes, we found supplies like food, medical supplies, and weapons. There were many kinds of cases of penicillin and other drugs. Sometimes, we found hair spray, pantyhose, and mostly menthol cigarettes. When we went down to any village, the women were always looking for them. Củ Chi had no local village, just some tiny houses. Their houses were made out of cardboard and flattened coke or beer cans they used for the walls. The roofs were made of thatched trees and branches.

I did over three tours in Vietnam, and I saw and did plenty. When I was assigned to the 4th Cav, I was with The Headquarters Troop, an intelligence operations unit. All officers reported directly to the commander, who was Major General Keith Ware. He was awarded the Medal of Honor from the battle in Normandy during World War ll. His call sign was 66. My forward observation team consisted of our officer, he was called Dragoon 24. Our Sergeant was called 24 Romeo.

19

I was the Radio Man, and my call sign was 24 Kilo. At that time, I was a Specialist 4.

The 4th Cav was a full-out assault and quick-moving outfit. We had M48 and M60 tanks, and M113 armored personnel carrier. Each one of them had a 50-caliber machine gun and a M60 machine gun on the side. We also had at least two Zippo tracks, which we called flame throwers. We also had the LRRPs with us. There were mostly Huey helicopters and IJHI B choppers - no doors with miniguns or Gatling guns attached to each door. Some only had M60 machine guns. The Gatling guns could fire 300 rounds a minute. Some of the choppers were fitted with rockers attached to the guns on the doors and some attached to the front of the gunship.

Most of the time that I was with the 4th Cav, we were in the field 90% of the time. Sometimes, we got to go down to the local village of Phu-Loi. Twenty dollars back then was enough to get drunk and get laid. Each little bar had about a dozen girls who would have sex with you for ten dollars. You had to be careful because the North Vietnam sympathizers would grind up glass and put it in a sandwich. Also, the hookers would slip razor blades in their vaginas. You had to be careful about what you were saying about any future operations. There were always gals around our barracks cleaning up and doing other menial tasks. Sometimes, they would be caught in our S-2 barracks, which had all our local maps hanging on the walls. Before any mission, we were all told where we were going. As soon as we got to the location where we were going, guess who showed up? Plenty of girls on little scooters carrying beer and cigarettes. The women would work in the rice fields even when they were pregnant. Sometimes, they would even have their babies and keep on working.

For most big operators, the whole division is involved in the operation. Sometimes, our outfit was called out to help other outfits that were under attack. On operation Birmingham, we were on our way to Täy Ninh, where the Michelin Rubber Plantation was located. While passing through Củ Chi, we were attacked by the regular north V.C. (Viet Cong). These guys were no mama's boys. We would fire napalm down the tunnel, and in about ten minutes, one of them would come up shooting. These guys could live one week on a handful of rice with a little fish. As we passed the tunnels, our commanding officer would drop hand grenades down them. One time he forgot to lean away, and the shrapnel hit him in the side of his butt. He told us not to tell anybody how he received his purple heart.

Eight

The Major Incident

Sometimes, we went down into the tunnels in CuChi to see what was there. We found all kinds of medical supplies, pantyhose, cigarettes, rice, and all kinds of drugs that the soldiers used to get rid of Malaria and other diseases we would get when we crossed the river separating us from Cambodia. Sometimes in the morning, before we went out to look for the V.C., we would say to each other 'today is a good day to die". The best soldiers were the street kids; they knew how to survive because they had done it back home. They knew they had nothing to lose, so they put their best foot forward every day. One day, the general's men went into Cambodia and asked if any regiments were coming but also told us that if we got caught, we were on our own. The government wasn't worried. We saw at least 3,000 enemies, some tanks but mostly small arms and plenty of RP-6s, which were armor-piercing rounds, and others mostly had AK-47 machine guns.

One time, in a firefight, a guy was manning the 50 calpur on an APG in combat. His your adrenaline is running at full speed, and when he grabbed a barrel to switch it out, the other both of them were hot as fire, and he burned both of his hands. They started dropping Agent Orange again into the jungle, which cleared all the foliage, but the residual stuff ended up in the river, where of course, we all drank from, and that's the most common way most of us soldiers got exposed.

One day, a new 2nd Lieutenant showed up to the unit. As a newly commissioned officer, I've spent a lot of time in a classroom, reading books and learning about military tactics from history. Young officers would show up overly confident and inexperienced. They gave the orders, but we knew the jungle. This Lieutenant was stubborn and was either too proud to admit it or too inexperienced to understand that his classroom training and rigorously structured battle plans that he learned thousands of miles away back in the US were not going to keep us alive here in Vietnam. Vietnam was different, it wasn't regular warfare, and we'd been seeing shit go down ever since we got here. He either did not understand or admit that he never went with the 1/4 Calvery regiment on maneuvers. He was going to take the company through CuChi, which was connected to all kinds of tunnel running ground. I told him if he went that way, he would lose too many people and that I was not going along because so many of them were my friends. He put me under house arrest for disobeying an order. When they took off, I listened in on the radio during their trip. They got ambushed, and a couple of armored personnel carriers and a couple of soldiers were lost in the ambush. When he got back, I told the military police that were guarding me to hand me a piece. I took the 45-caliber pistol and shot the Lieutenant in the knee. I was subsequently court marshaled, and as a punishment, they took my stripes 90% of my money.

Nine

Scorpion Warnings

One day, I was helping the artillery boys sandbag their guns and ammo when I lifted it up, a giant black and purple scorpion bit me. I went to the medics, and the doctor gave me a pill. The doctor said, "If you're still alive tomorrow, come back and see me." My right arm swelled up like a watermelon, but I eventually got through it. Another guy in my outfit got bit by a snake while we were traveling through bushes. It was small and green, and we called it the 2-step snake because after you get bit, you make two steps, and you're out. Right before you die, your eyes roll back, and your mouth overflows with white foam. Another day of chaos was watching someone swallow their tongue in a firefight. We tried helping him get it out but were not able to. A medic showed up, took out his knife, stuck it in the guy's tongue, and pulled it up. Another doctor in the field showed us how to do a tracheotomy, cut a slit in the throat, and use a straw to release air.

Every time our commander took his Chopper out, one of the forward observers had to go with him in case he crashed. On one mission, We were around the Seaport when we ran into a bunch of Sea Bees. They invited me in to have something to drink and eat. They ended up having plenty of Johnny Walker Red and Black. I asked them what they wanted to trade for it, and they said they had no ammo and wanted hand grenades, tear gas, flares, and small weapons shells. So I told the Colonel, who told me to take his slip, grab all our duffle bags, fill them up, and give it to the Sea Bees. When we did, they gave us back a load of booze. We filled our duffle bags to the brim and took them back to our guys in the field. So, the Captain said to give one bag to the mess sergeant, supply sergeant, and any other supply units with us, including the artillery commander. I just divided the rest out to anybody, including the gunship pilots and their crews.

I remember the time we were on a patrol by the Cambodian Border, we ran into a whole regiment of Viet Cong soldiers, and we had to run into the river and stay hidden for three days. Our bodies were covered in leeches and bugs. Not everyone was tough like most of us. One guy almost gave our location away because he started to panic from all the bugs crawling on us. I had to remind him how quickly we all will die if he doesn't get it together.

After we did our jobs, we returned to Phu-Lui, our base. Much of our time was spent filling fill water bags and other kinds of boring stuff. They used to come to our barracks looking for forward observers.

The F.O's duty was to call in air strikes and fire missions using artillery batteries. We had F-4 jets back then, and our artillery suits that went with us were packed with the necessary manpower. We never used our real names. We went by code names for fire missions. My code name was Dragon 24 Kilo. Anytime I fired a mission, I announced, "This is a 24-kilo fire mission".

We could have been out there for 30 days, but the politicians wouldn't let us do our job. Before we fired on any enemy, we had to get clearance to see if they were friendly. You couldn't trust anyone or go with your gut. Anyone could walk up with a hat, black pajamas, and an AK-47 at his side. And you'd better be ready to do something.

Ten

The Attack

Once on our way to Täy Ninh, we were attacked on the road with small arms fire and RPGs, which were known as armored piercing rockets. If they hit a tank or a 113 personal carrier, it could burn through eight inches of solid steel. The M48 tank in front of us hit a 5,000-pound bomb that never detonated. Dropped by one of our B52 bombers. It blew the turret completely off the tank, exposing us to small-arms fire. My tank commander was wounded, and so were two others who were on the tank. So, I immediately called a dust-off helicopter to pick up our wounded comrades.

While the shooting was going on, three kids ran up to the side of my tank. The person in the rear hatch had a M60 machine gun and mowed them down. We had no choice because they were carrying hand grenades with AK47 Russian machine guns. When their bodies were flying back to the ground, I could see the bullet holes across their chests. When they hit the ground, they never made a sound. They just closed their eyes and died. I'll never forget how tough they were.

The tank in front of us got hit so hard that one of our guys almost had his head blown off. As we were still engaged in the battle, this guy got up and ran the 100-yard dash with no head, blood gushing out the top of his head coming from his neck. Finally, he dropped down. All that was pretty scary. I will never forget that as long as I live.

Finally, the medevac choppers came and rescued our wounded troopers. The guys had the red cross emblems painted on the helicopters. The Viet Cong couldn't care less. They still tried to shoot them down, knowing that they would not return fire. The U.S. Forces always tried to comply with the Geneva Conventions. The Viet Cong, however, were being supplied by the Russians. All their weapons were Russian-made. Their machine guns were AK47's. Their mortars were one millimeter bigger than our 4.2 mortars. Meaning they could use our shells to fire in their guns.

After this little incursion was over, we continued on to Tây Ninh and Vinh Phúc Province, which were southwest of Saigon. There, we were attacked again by a small band of around 40-60 V.C. soldiers. As one of our tanks was engaging it, we got hit on the track. Our repair guys were training to reinstall a new track and make repairs. We watched them try to reinstall a new section of track. They laid the four-foot sections on the ground and didn't hold them up to give them tension before they drove the long bouts that held them together. As soon as the tank made a sharp turn, the track came flying off. The tank commander asked them where they went to school. All he did was shake his head with bewilderment.

Sometimes, we were close to the Cambodian River, where the V.C. was located. So, while we were on our side, we had orders not to cross across the river. Night after night and even during the daytime, they would monitor us. After about a week, our Commanding Officer called us on headsets and said I've had enough of this bullshit. I'm crossing the river. Whoever wants to go with me, saddle up. We were all the wild bunch, so we all went with him, knowing we could all get court martialed. We were about three clicks away from going into Cambodia when we got a call from 66, who was our Commanding General. He said get your ass's back to our side of the river so he could explain our situation. We couldn't cross the river according to U.S. involvement in Vietnam.

On our way through Tây Ninh province, we were attacked with small arms fire, but within minutes, they were gone. The trees around us were usually rubber trees. Our track bumped into one, and a thousand red ants came down on all of us. We tried using the spray the army gave us, but it didn't kill them. It seemed it made them madder, so everybody started taking off their clothes to get rid of the ants. We were all laughing because if we got shot at, nobody was at the guns or rifles.

In the field, we had to take salt pills because of the heat. Sometimes it got up to 120-130. We had our helmets on plus our flap jackets on, plus our web gear, in which we carried our canteens, knives, hand grenades, and other supplies. Any time we had to get water from other sources, we had to put quinine tablets in the water and boil it for about thirty minutes. After any mission, when we returned to base, the first thing we did was fuel up our tanks and other tracks. We made sure we had plenty of ammo. Then, if we had time, we would go to our little Post Exchange to get supplies. We would look for canned goods, hygiene items, cigarettes, or other goodies.

Once, when we were filling up, one soldier was backed in by an M48 tank. He was caught between a concrete wall, and the tanker couldn't see him. He was killed instantly. On another day, one of our radio repair guys was in a 113 track trying to fix a PRC 25 radio. Whatever he did, he shorted out something, and some of the shells started exploding, and he was killed.

Sometimes, we got to stand down for a few days. We mostly wrote letters home, played cards, and drank a lot of beer. Every now and then, we got recruits in because we lost plenty of our guys. About half the guys that were assigned to us never went home. When we were really drunk, we would practice throwing our knives. One of us would stand by the wall and spread eagle. Each guy got five throws at us from about 15 feet away. Once, they struck me in the right hand, which I had to get stitched up. Then I took my turm, and we all just laughed. We would ask the new guys if they wanted to play, and they responded by telling us we were all crazy. We just told them we weren't crazy; we just weren't afraid.

Our outfit had A, B, and C troops, which were made up of tanks and armored personnel carriers. Delta was attached to us; they were the LRRP's. Long range reconnaissance patrol, we had our own gunships. Everywhere we went, the headquarters troop went with them. We had Sl and S2 intelligence with our surveyors and forward observers, which I was a part of even though we went behind them. We were frequently got and exposed to danger. One of my good friends was killed — he drove the lead tank for us. Either the captain, the sergeant, or I always went with any squadron that went out. Usually, when the General flew, one of us had to go with him in case his chopper went down. Once, his chopper was taking off, and the rudder caught the barbed wire along the airstrip. Before we could get him on the radio, the chopper's rotary blade hit first, and the chopper rolled over. We ran up and pulled out the pilot, the door gunner, and the General.

Eleven

Christmas on the front

During Operation Cedar Falls, I remember on Thanksgiving Day the Chinook helicopters brought us turkey, dressing and all the fixings for a Thanksgiving dinner. I can say one thing about the military I don't care where we were they took care of us. I think we had a cease fire for three days. That year when Christmas came around we were entertained by having Bob Hope, Joey Heatherton, Martha Roy, and Henry Fonda. When Henry Fonda came through our barracks we got to see him without any makeup on. He looked about 30 years older than he was. That week our General at that time was General Depuy. Most of our division had most units there. The General said to all of us if anybody here doesn't want to be here raise your hand and I will send you home with a honorable discharge. Not one soldier raised his hand even though everybody complained a lot. When it came down to it, nobody wanted to be called chicken.

Before the Tet Offensive started the General asked for three volunteers to go across the river to see if we could find any of the North V.C. gathering and what kind of units they were. He also said those who go, if caught, the U.S. would say they had no knowledge of our whereabouts. He also said we probably wouldn't have much of a chance to get back. Me and two others volunteered on our way back and came into contact with a V.C. regiment. So, we went into the river to wait for a chance to escape. In those three days, we had water and some C-rations to sustain ourselves. The only thing bad was we had leeches and snakes all around us. We did have a radio which we later used to call a helicopter to get back to base. Then most of our unit was positioned around Saigon.

Our country dropped thousands of leaflets telling the local people to make sure they were off the street by 6 pm. The week that we thought the attack was coming, we were told to shoot anybody that was outside. Our own troops that were in the rear came out to us to buy souvenirs from us. Our division was off units in Saigon because they figured we were too dangerous. Most of them didn't even know what was going on around them.

Twelve

Rumors of my death are greatly exaggerated

After my first year was almost up, they made us stand down for about two weeks. One night, I was in bed waiting to go to Hong Kong for my ten days of leave, and another soldier was three weeks away from being discharged. He was scared to go on a two-day patrol around the base, so I said I would go, and he took my duty. We never switched the duty roster. Days later, he got blown away so severely they couldn't identify his body. Before I got my orders to get on the plane, they checked us for carrying drugs, weapons, or any other contraband. We also had to piss test while we still had about three days to go home. They wanted to make sure we did not have any venereal disease. I heard one guy had green balls that were about 6 to 8 inches blown up. All the guys that were going home were kept together and guarded by military police. When I got back to Travis Air Base, they were unloading our buddies in their coffins covered with the American flag. We also saw the hippies and protesters burning our flags and spitting at the police. We all wished we could have had five minutes with these guys.

When I got home and knocked on the door, my older brother Gaw answered the door and closed it in my face. I knocked again, and he opened it, stunned, and said, "Is it really you?" I said, "Yes, it's me,

Bruce, your brother." He was still in shock as he told me they sent a telegram to Mom and Dad saying I was killed in combat. They dropped a nuclear bomb, and no one survived. Dad kept saying he couldn't believe it and told my brother and sisters if they dropped a nuclear bomb and one soldier came out alive, it would be me. Then I told him what happened, so he went to get some beer and wild turkey. We sat down to have a drink, and I looked at my dad and told him he wasn't as dumb son of a bitch as I thought he was. He just laughed and said now you know. As he walked away, I asked my mother why we never got along. She answered me by saying, when he looks at you, he's looking in the mirror at himself. When she married my dad, he only had a motorcycle and a pair of boots when she was pregnant with me. She said I was just as stubborn as my father and had to learn things the hard way. After that day, my dad and I were the best of friends. He knew I finally grew up.

Every day that I was home, I always wore my uniform. I went to bars mainly looking for protestors, and sometimes I found them. One night, I was drinking until 2:00 am, and after that I went to eat breakfast. I was pretty drunk, and I dropped my fork, and a booth of four punks were laughing at me. They said don't they teach you guys how to use utensils? So, I got up and said, "What's that?" One jumped up, and I took the sugar container and smashed it into his face. The rest got up, but they were no match for me. I stuck one of them and stuck his head in the jukebox. Another one I shoved through the plate glass window. All of a sudden, the police showed up and handcuffed me. While we were waiting for the shore patrol, the four guys kept yelling at the cops to take me to jail. One officer got irritated and asked them, have any of you been arrested? They said no and were not going to be. The officer walked behind me and, uncuffed me and told them to get in the police car. I asked the officer to give me five minutes with them. He said I wish I could, so he told me to take off. The owner came out and told me there was about $3,000 in damage. All of a sudden, an old Marine came up to me and said if he were 40 years younger, he would have jumped in. He not only paid my bill but invited me to his home to meet his family.

Another time, I was leaving a topless joint. I guess I was doing about 70 mph before I even got on the freeway. The policeman who pulled me over had a nephew in the service, so he gave me a break. He made me follow him to a 24-hour coffee shop. He told me he got off duty in six hours, and my car had better still be parked there. One night, some of my friends came over to play cards. My friend Manual was in the Marines when I was there. I guess I got up out of my chair in the kitchen and slammed my dad against the wall. I pulled my k-bar knife, and I was going to kill him. Manual grabbed my arm and stopped me. He told my dad I didn't realize I was home and thought I was back in Vietnam. The next day, my dad told me he thought I was playing around and said I scared him out.

Another day, I spotted my neighbor outside my dad's house. I was still dressed in my khakis, and he asked if we could get caught up. I was naturally down to relax and catch up. He went inside and got some beers and tequila, and we just sat on the porch talking. Shortly after, a car of guys slowly drove by and threw a bunch of bottles on my dad's lawn. I yelled for them to turn around and come pick it up. They stopped, and I saw about five guys in the car yelling back at me. I said you want to fight? Go get all your friends and meet me in the street. So I went back to my dad's house, grabbed his M-1 Carbine he had brought back from WWII, and met those hooligans in the street. Not long after, the sheriff arrived and instantly noticed me, "Bruce? Is that you? Didn't you just get back today??" I said, "Yes." He then replied, "Say Hi to your mom and dad for me, and remember, if you kill anybody, make sure it's on your property." One of the troublemakers remembered me at that point and told the rest of them to leave and not come back because "Bruce will kill all of us."

Thirteen

Back again

One reason I kept going back to Vietnam was when I came home on leave and saw all the college boys protesting the war and burning our flags. We saw people spitting on our police and just a bunch of rowdy kids. Soon, I was back on the plane headed back to Vietnam. We stopped in Alaska, then went on to Guam, where the B52s were everywhere. I was sitting on the plane in my uniform and had a few medals and ribbons. Many new guys going over for the first time came up to me with their orders to ask me where they were being assigned. Most of them were non-combatants and had no combat experience at boot camp. Some guys were infantry, so I told them where they were going. They asked me plenty of questions about combat. I told them when the bullets started flying to hit the ground, count to ten and have a cigarette. I told them not to panic, focus, and listen to their platoon leaders.

One of the most extensive operations for our division was called Junction City. This operation was set up to try to find out what was going on before the Tet Offensive. Usually, when we left our home base, we went through to Lai-Kai, which contained a lot of artillery units with 105 howitzers. They also had an airstrip where we got supplies and could land our choppers. After that, we headed to Zion, where more of our division was located. The most famous highway in Vietnam was called Highway One. Any time we headed through Cu-Chi province, we could expect trouble. When We got around the Cambodian border, we usually came in contact with the enemy. We usually had an artillery unit with us every time we made camp. Our tanks and APC's armored personnel carriers would encircle us just like the covered wagons did in the old days. We usually helped the boys sandbag their guns and helped them with their ammo in case we had a combat situation.

Sometimes, we would be mortared by the enemy at night. They did it just to mess with us. Usually, when they mortared us, they landed them five in a row. I would wait until the second round hit to run out and try to find the fin in the ground so I could take an azimuth to locate their position by using my plumb-bop. If I had a good idea, I would call a fire mission and shoot a few rounds back at them. The next day, we would go to the area where we sent the rounds. Sometimes, we found nothing, and sometimes we found a few dead V.C.

One night, we were really being hit hard. I was with the headquarters troop attached to B-Squadron. The Captain and the Sergeant weren't with me. The Captain of B Troop told me to get them off our back. So, I called in the coordinates to almost come right on top of us. I told everybody to button up because it was coming. It came so close our track was bouncing. The Captain said that was close enough. Sometimes, we had a squadron of Rock soldiers attached to us. These guys were some tough sons of bitches. All they did was shine their knives and do exercises all day. I'm glad we didn't have to fight them.

Once, we were on some bridge, and there were about six prisoners. Our Officers were questioning them without any results, but when the Rock Commander questioned them, and they wouldn't talk, they just shot them in the head and pushed them over the bridge. By the time they got to the third prisoner, he started telling them what we wanted to know. After some of our battles, the Chinooks would fly in to get our dead guys out. One of the worst things we had to do was to load the body bags on them. Naturally, we knew that could be any of us. We had some chinooks that were used by dropping flares to light up our surrounding positions. They were called the Jolly Green Giants. They were rigged with gantline guns on both sides of the chopper. There were four doors, and believe me, when they fired, every 7th round was a red tracer round. They shot so fast it looked like a steady stream of red.

On one operation of Operation Junction City, we were on our way southwest to Täy Ninh, which was close to the Cambodian border. We were about five days into our destination when we made camp. At night, sometimes, we would make three-man teams to go out on the perimeter to set trip flares and claymore mines in case the enemy were close. We used very thin wire, which was called trip wire. As we were almost done, one of our own guys set off the wire and lit up the area. We just looked at each other and laughed because if there were any enemies out there, we would all be dead. In another episode, we were on a three-day patrol. This time, we had one of our troops with us. Charlie Troop, which we called C Troop, had about fourteen tanks, a couple of armored personnel carriers, and one of the infantry units that came with us. When we got back to our area, one of our guys drove his tank up to the mess truck. He knocked on the door, and the mess sergeant responded by saying it was only three o'clock in the morning. Come back at 6 am, and you can eat with everybody else. So, this guy jumped back in his tank, drove up to the truck and lowered his gun, and told the Sergeant you have two minutes to get his ass off the truck. Then he said, if I can't eat, nobody else is going to either. Then he blew up the truck. They made him re-enlist for three years to pay for the truck.

In the monsoon season, it rains like folly days and forty nights. One night out in my little pump tent, I was trying to sleep when I felt something walking up my stomach. When I opened my eyes, I was looking at big red eyes. I almost jumped out of my skin when I realized it was just a big water rat. He was only trying to get out of the rain, too. You didn't know what to expect out in the jungle, from banana snakes to scorpions.

After any battle while in the field, our doctor, who was a surgeon, would walk around to look at some of the wounded to see who needed attention according to their wounds. I saw one guy on the medivac chopper who had an M79 grenade shell stuck in his stomach. We told him if it didn't spin, it wouldn't explode. We all carried these needles that contained morphine, and when somebody was wounded, we could just hit them anywhere, and the needle would inject by itself. Some guys went into shock that weren't hurt that bad, and they died. One of the worst things I saw was somebody swallowed their tongue. No one knew what to do. We were lucky a medic happened to be there. He took a piece of wire, stuck it through his tongue, and pulled it up. This guy was turning blue before he pulled his tongue up.

Fourteen

Lucky Luciano's daughter

After my second trip home, I was hanging around San Francisco at a stop sign, and a random chick opened my passenger door and hopped in. She looked at me, still in uniform, and asked, "You looking for some girls to have a good time with? If so, take me home, and when I come out, I'll show you where to look". Hours later, we ended up at a nightclub, and the first thing I noticed were several men dressed in tuxedos. Not much happened there; the night started off pretty blandly. The next club we went to, I noticed the same guys there in tuxedos. I jokingly asked if she knew those men, and she casually mentioned them as her bodyguards. I was stunned and looked at her in disbelief. I asked her, "Well, what's your name??" she responded shyly, "Oh, I am Lucky Luciano's daughter.

I was shocked, but we were already out, and I thought, let's have fun. The next day, she said let's go to the courthouse, and I'll show you something really funny, and we did. We entered without any hassles, even though she had a pistol in her purse. I just thought being the daughter of Lucky's must go a long way because she wasn't even stopped to be patted down. Turns out she went to law school and bailed out a bunch of people who were tried unfairly, mostly prostitutes. However, she was a lovely lady that I befriended and would send me postcards when I returned back to duty.

Fifteen

The Third Tour

When it came time for my third tour in Vietnam, I went to Hong Kong. Naturally, we went to all the places they told us were off-limits. I went to Kowloon, a small province in Hong Kong. At the time, it was governed by the British. Naturally, we went to the bars looking for girls and to have a good time. I was staying at the Grand Hotel. We were just a bunch of guys from all branches of the service sitting down to have breakfast. They had a buffet, just like the military. While we were eating, one of the British Navy Soldiers made a comment to one of our Marine buddies. He said, "What's the matter with you Yanks? Why are you getting your asses kicked"? I jumped up and said I didn't know about the rest of the guys, but I'm not going to put up with this bullshit. Before you know it, we all got up and started World War III. Pretty soon, here came the military police, and they stopped us. They didn't want to arrest anybody, so we all chipped in to pay the bill. After that, we all shook hands, said we were our allies and laughed. Then, we all went on our merry way.

At one bar, I met a girl who helped the bartender. She didn't drink, and she wasn't a local hooker. I asked her to have lunch with me before I went back to Vietnam, so she gave me her address. I took a cab to her residence, and to my surprise, her house looked like a mansion. Before approaching her front door, I asked the taxi driver who she was. He

43

told me her father was some kind of Ambassador. So, her parents came out to greet me. They wanted to know about the war and what was going on. We were all told not to talk or discuss anything about our units or anything. After I returned back to the base, I stayed in contact by writing a few letters.

So, during my three and a half tours, I went to Hong Kong twice, Kuala Lumpur, Malaysia, and back home. I served under three different generals in the three biggest campaigns, including Cedar Falls, Junction City, and Birmingham. They also rotated every year like everybody else. They were: 1st General Hays, 2nd General Depuy, 3rd Major General Keith Ware, and 4th General Tallbort.

I am not sure about the other outfits, but our outfit was not allowed to visit any local spots like Vung Tao and other rest areas where other soldiers got to get a couple of weeks' break in the action. I guess our unit was too dangerous to give passes to. I was surprised by the guys in the rear areas who really didn't know what was going on. We had orders not to even get out of our vehicles because we were all packing weapons and other gear. In my opinion, a lot of the guys that were missing in action took off or just stayed with the local people. Probably before being in the service, they had no social life or friends because they came from foster homes or broken homes.

On one of our operations close to the border of Southwest Cambodia, we got overran by a small group of Viet Cong. So, as we ducked down, to our surprise, when they overran our positions, they just kept on going. All we had to do was to stand up and kill them. They were so stoned that they were probably just told to attack us and keep going. On another operation, when we were headed up north, we crossed trails with the 11th Cav. The old man called all of us to put on our yellow scarves that had our 4th Cav insignia embossed on them, which were bright yellow. The 11th Cav's colors were white and red.

Another time, we were on a mission in the jungle with some units of the 196th Infantry Division. They had the wolf hounds with them. Most of them were German Shepard's. They only took commands from the soldier who was in charge of them. One night, I went to get a cup of coffee, and as I passed one of them, he jumped right at me. The only thing that stopped him was a one-inch chain that had him held to a tree. The dogs were trained to sniff out explosive devices like claymore mines or trip flares. If one of the trainers got killed, they had to kill the dog because they wouldn't take commands from anybody. On one flight home, we had to chain one guy to his seat. He was barking like a dog.

Sixteen

Return Home

When I still had four months to go, I tried to volunteer for a fourth tour, but the General said I had done enough already. Still, I got to stay an extra three months as one of our Tankers only had two weeks to go, so I switched duty with him. He was an artilleryman by trade. A short time later, I was discharged from the army. One month after I came home, General Ware's helicopter crashed, and he was killed. During World War II, he was awarded the Congressional Medal of Honor.

Even after I was discharged from the service, I still wore my uniform when I went drinking. I spent the first few weeks looking up some of my old school buddies. I found out pretty soon that the people in our country did not really know what was going on. It seemed that all our friends didn't want to associate with us. One of my good friends was in our division attached to the 2nd of the 28th Infantry. I found out that he had stepped on a land mine and got killed. His family didn't live that far from my house, so I went to visit his mother and his family. All I could tell the mom was that he didn't suffer.

All I can remember is when I got home I had a lot of rage inside me after watching the protestors burning our flags and causing problems with the soldiers and the local police department. I joined a karate class and a few bowling leagues. While hanging out in the studio, the owner asked me why I wanted to learn from him. He said he knew who I was and said you're a pretty good street fighter. So, I told him even when I win, I look like the loser.

I went to visit one of my school buddies named Buzzy Fontaine. His family owned a local glass company in San Jose, and we also went to the same High School. When we were still in High School, we were working on his Jeep when one of the fan blades broke off, hitting him in the face. He was so big that he covered the cut with his hand while I drove him to the hospital, where they stitched him up. Now, here we were. I returned from war, and Buzz was in the Military Police (M-P).

Seventeen

Watsonville

After Vietnam, I lived in Watsonville and joined The National Guard to see if our boys were getting trained okay. So when I went in to see the Post Commander, he just looked at my discharge papers and said, "Was there anything you didn't do?" jokingly. They had a two week drill in Hunter Legget where they had M48 and M60 tanks and a few armored personal carriers. They were showing them by the book if they had a round that didn't go off. The book said to wait 15 minutes and get rid of it. The Capitan said, "Bruce, go ahead and tell them what to do if it happens in combat." I told them straight like it is, "You don't have time, just grab it and toss it, and take your chances." "Same thing with the M72 Law Rocket Launcher. You don't have time to bury it; just pick it up and break it off on a tree to get rid of it, too." I also told them not to look at the light when they turn the tank lights on. It has 1000 candle power and easily blinds you. So they made me a Tank Commander.

I remember asking the Captain why no one ate in the Mess Hall, and he said no one liked the food. When the Mess Sergeant retired, they told me I could take the job and earn my Sergeant Stripes back quickly. The food they provided was alright, but the book didn't allow them to improvise. So I started off with hamburger meat and sent two guys to the store to get tomato sauce, ribs, and Italian sausage. I made spaghetti and meatballs that night. For dessert, I had a friend from Watsonville bring fresh strawberries from his farm, and I made a strawberry short-cake. I used red and white tablecloths with a checkerboard pattern and fixed the Mess Hall up a little. The Captain came down with a couple of soldiers who were shocked to see how I turned the place around.

Everyone was curious as to how I learned to cook, and I told them briefly my dad was a decorated soldier who didn't just kill people. Days he was in the jungle with his outfit, they had no food or fresh water, so they used a small pot over the fire and threw anything that moved into it. Sometimes, they got a hold of wild chickens, and he told his guys that once he got out of the jungle and headed back home, he would never eat another chicken in his life. He never did. My dad taught himself how to cook by taste and winging all his measurements to his liking. It was one of the few things I learned from him. My dad was also very strict about food; he always told us whatever he put on our plates had better go into our bodies. He was also a big fan of bread and butter and always told my mom to make sure it was always on the table for dinner.

I knew my dad was a decorated soldier because I saw the cases his medals came in, but he never talked about it. In those days, they called it shell shock, but it was actually Post Traumatic Disorder from war. He couldn't sleep unless he had enough beers. When they all came home there were a lot of guys that were on the death march. They had to tie them down because most of them tried jumping off the ship. We all hoped it wouldn't happen again, but then Korea and Vietnam came up, and here we went again. That's why I kept going back to Nam any chance I could get. I wanted to make sure my dad was proud of me. I wanted him to know I was a soldier, a good one at that. I wanted to make him proud to talk about me if he ever did.

When I got home from Nam, I went to church, and when the min-ister asked if anyone had anything to say after his service, I raised my hand to speak. I don't recall exactly what I said, but it was the time of Christmas, and they mentioned that we had to give the church money. I told them I disagreed with this because no one can buy their way into heaven. I told them there were a lot of them that bought their sons way out of going. Only us regular people went, and I told them shame on all of you. The minister did tell me that it is good for you to tell people the truth. However, when I got home, all I did was go to bars and was hardly ever home. I went out to bars looking for girlfriends. I never had one to write to or go home to when I was a soldier.

When I went out, I usually wore black clothes like Johnny Cash and always sat at the end of the bars. I remember the night a few girls asked the bartender if there was anywhere they could sit without creepy men hitting on them. The bartender looked down the bar at me and said, "Go sit next to that guy; that's where you want to sit if you want to just enjoy yourselves. I guarantee you no one will mess with you if you sit next to that man." So they did, and no one bothered them. They went back to the bartender to ask "who is he?" He replied, "That guy went to Nam three or four times and has seen it all. He ain't afraid of nobody; just stick by him." I eventually got too drunk, and they actually had to drive me home, but we ended up at the bartender's house, where I slept in the front. The next day, I treated everyone to dinner on Santa Cruz Beach, where we all hung out and enjoyed each other's company. After that, we all became good friends and stayed in touch.

There was another time I went out to eat at a local restaurant where a family of five was having dinner, and I saw the man smack his wife across the face in front of their children. I got up and walked over to their table and punched him in the face, and told her not to put up with this crap in front of your kids. She said she was scared to leave and told her she could get a restraining order at the police station and go away.

There was another time I was coming back from Santa Cruz, and there was a two car crash blocking the highway. I pulled over and took my flares out to help light the scene. I arrived just in time because it was so dark. There was a gas tanker coming down at high speed, and when he saw the lit flares, he was able to slam the breaks just in time. When I got to the people in the accident, one lady had broken her ankle and had minor bruises and cuts, and I told her not to look at her injuries. She was okay and going to be just fine, and the ambulance was already on its way. One of the essential things being in combat was not to let anyone go into shock. Keeping everyone alert during any kind of injury sustained during combat was vital to surviving. When the cop arrived, he was relieved that I had helped save him a ton of paperwork from the accident. I told him the only thing I needed was my flares, and he walked me back to his patrol car and gave me a case of his flares.

Eighteen

Battle Scars

After I was home for about a month, I decided to try to find a job. We all went to the unemployment office to get unemployment insurance. We had to fill out papers and see an agent. He asked us what kind of work we were looking for. One guy told him he was a Harpooner on a whaling ship. Another told him he was an Orchestra Conductor, and the agent announced he would not help us. A manager, with one arm missing, came over to us. He was a Korean War Vet. So, he told the lady to pay us. He said I know all you guys just want drinking money to get drunk.

Most of the Nam Vets kind of stuck together. Many of us tried reconnecting with our High School friends, but they didn't want to talk to us. My friends would tell me that when I got drunk, I turned into Frankenstein. My buddy was a door gunner in Nam, but we came home, and he didn't act the same way anymore. He told me he had enough killing in Vietnam and told me I got worse. I found that most of the guys in action didn't want to go there anymore.

One of my friends and I went night clubbing. When we were parking our car, we saw a guy just beating up a girl in the parking lot. We jumped out, and he took off. I went to the girl and put my jacket over her. All the people at the bar were just outside, watching what was happening. I said to them weren't any of you going to stop the guy.

They replied they were all afraid of getting involved. That night, as we were leaving, some guy pulled a gun on me. I told him to shoot. You might blow my hand off, but also, you will blow your face apart.

All my life after the war was over, I was always looking for these kind of people. They are the ones who don't give the older people on buses their seats and make them stand up. Also, they are the ones that play their music too loud, but when I was around them, I told them you people want to deal with me? I told them, "Do you want to dance with the devil in the pale moonlight?

One time, I was working in Seattle, and I was in another restaurant. There were about four young guys in there eating their breakfast. They kept looking at me, so I went up to them and told them, you boys don't scare me. I told them all, did you ever shit in your pants? They looked up at me and asked me why I said that. Boys, if you've never done that, then you don't know what scared is. One guy looked at me and said you're crazy and I said, "No If you punks were with us in Vietnam, you would keep your mouths shut." They just got on their motorcycles and left.

Nineteen

Finding Love

The whole time I was in Vietnam, I never really had a steady girlfriend. This all changed one night after I returned. I was out with some friends, and I kept looking at this one lady who caught my attention. I knew she was a little older than me, but I didn't care. She was 43, and I was only 21. I ended up following her around until she went out with me, and soon after that, we got married. I was soon to find out that she had been married three times already, but I was in love, and off we went to Reno. She had three children, a daughter who was 17 and two sons who were 9 and 13.

I took up a job as a plasterer to support the family, and one day, when the machine that I used broke down, I went to my wife's job to surprise her and take her out to lunch. I went to her office, and somebody said she had gone somewhere with her boss. While I was waiting in the parking lot, they came driving up in a limo. So, I didn't bother them. I just went back home. Later, I found out she was messing around with one of the local police officers in the area. Soon after that, we split up after barely a year together.

Twenty

Cathy

My second wife was a bartender back in the 70s. That was the time hot pants were in style. After my first marriage, I started taking karate lessons from a local studio. After I told him that, he said he would teach me. We got to be good friends, so I started to hang around with him quite a bit. She was washing her glasses, and she dropped one in the sink and cut her finger while all the other guys in the bar were laughing. I left for Walgreens to get her some bandages, brought them back to her, and went home. The next day, she was asking around who I was. People said they weren't sure but knew my karate teacher was Ralph Castellanos. He owned Castys Kenpo. Ralph was dating one of the waitresses and one night, they were out having a good time. A bunch of guys kept harassing his wife for a dance while Ralph stepped in the back. I told them to back off and let them enjoy their meal in peace, and we could go outside and talk. So I went outside with 5 of them and when someone told Ralph he said: "Oh Bruce doesn't need my help, just five guys? He's good". But Ralph sent someone out there, and the guys left. Guess they didn't want to get their asses handed to them.

The next time I saw Cathy, I asked her out to the movies. Cathy showed up at my house with a six year old girl named Serena. I went to take a shower, and Cathy came in and took her clothes off. You could say we never made it to the movies. She seemed to be the one I was looking for. Soon after that, we started dating, and about three months later, we were married and had two children together, girls named Sharee and Shannon.

We moved to Watsonville and bought a house. It was in Watsonville that I launched my ice cream business. I leased about ten trucks from a guy in San Jose. One of the guys who helped us get our home asked why I didn't just buy the trucks since I was already paying 60% on leases; I might as well own them. He then asked how much I would need, and I told him about $60,000, as I also required a giant walk-in freezer. He told me we could get the money if I just paid interest on the house for three years. I can then refinance the house and pay off the $60,000.

Most of the drivers I hired were ex-cons. The patrol officers said to go to talk to Bruce. So when I hired people like that, I told them not to steal from me, and we wouldn't have a problem. I also told them if they ever got into any trouble to make sure they come to me and tell me what was going on. I told them all that my 357 Smith and Wesson was on me and all 12 of my ears from Nam. Throughout all my years in business, I have never had any problems with any of them. I like to look at it as me giving them a second chance at life. It felt good to give that back to these guys.

Life was not always perfect, though. At this point, Cathay was working at a golf course. One day, I went to pick her up and accused her of flirting with the customers. On the way home, I stopped at the golf course, we argued, and I slapped her upside the head. When we got home, I got my two 357 magnums and went on the couch to sleep. In the meantime, my wife called the police because she was scared of me. They went to the kids' bedroom to get the kids out of the window. While outside, they asked my daughters if I was a Veteran. They told the police I had done many tours in Vietnam and that I was a sniper. Then one cop told the other cop, "How do I get these kinds of cases?".

They were going to kick the front doors in to get my guns away from me. My older brother was a Sheriff, and he told the city police,

"Just let him sleep it off" because if you wake him up, he's not scared of you. You might have to kill him because he's not afraid of you, and he will take a lot of you with him. If you just leave him alone, he will wake up and won't remember anything.

Life was okay back then, but the wife and I never gave up on our drinking and socializing. One day, we were out drinking, and my daughter was babysitting when somebody tried to break into my brother-in-law's house and attacked my daughter. This terrified our family, and Cathy demanded to go back to Colorado. So we moved back there and bought another house. I went to work for a car dealer, and Cathy was a salesperson. I told her I wasn't happy and wanted to return to San Jose and that she and the kids should stay. Every two weeks or so, I would drive back and forth only to visit for 10 hours or so. As time went on, two weeks turned into longer gaps, and the visits got shorter. My daughters by now were 12 and 14 and Serena was 16. As much as I wanted to be there for them, I just was not able to make it happen. After about six months, Cathy told me it was okay to get a divorce, so I moved back in with my mother for a few years.

Twenty-One

Odd Jobs

Following my divorce, I started drinking a lot. Before too long, I met another girl, and we got married. However, it was not to last. One night, we got so drunk that we ended up in Reno, Nevada. Then, I found out she was an alcoholic. So we were only married for about three months. Shortly thereafter, one of my good old friends, John Gullo, who had moved to Seattle, WA, asked me to come work for him as a dispatcher for the mechanics. I took him up on the offer and stayed at one of the local hotels there until I could afford something better.

I was driving one day and saw a girl hitchhiking, and I picked her up. I asked her if she had run away from home, and she gently nodded. I asked her if she was hungry, and she said yes. So I took her to the hotel I was staying at after I took her to breakfast for food. I asked the manager at the hotel to help get this girl a place to stay for the month. When I went back to tell her, she was surprised and questioned my actions. I told her it was no funny business. I have daughters and would want someone like me to help them if anything happened to them. I got in touch with a local social worker and told them about the girl. They were able to help her and provide her with a job. Her social worker thanked me for helping out a girl I didn't know or have to help. She was in good hands now.

Another time I was in Seattle, I walked into a bar, and a guy was blocking the door so nobody could get in or out. This guy was a door gunner in Vietnam. He used to shoot drugs into his eyes to get high, and the bartender told me to help get him to calm down. He said he didn't want to have to call the police because he really wasn't that bad of a guy. So I approached him and told him I was in Nam too, and I knew exactly how he felt. I have been there and lived it all. We come back home from war and try to live our everyday lives, but it is a constant struggle. Life back here is not normal for us anymore. There were times I wanted to go to Berkeley and shoot people who were burning our flag. The disrespect enraged me, but I had to control myself because these ignorant people didn't know what we had to endure. Eventually, we were able to diffuse the situation, and everyone was able to leave safely.

My life, however, failed to improve. I kept getting caught driving and getting D.U.I. tickets. My drinking and gambling problems caused me only trouble with the police and local authorities. I used to wake up in the mornings in the forest where I went drinking. Before too long, I had lost my job and was left with just my old Volvo station wagon, so I decided to move back in with my mother in San Jose. I told her not to worry about me, and then if any of the bills came to give them to me, I would take care of them.

At one of my birthday parties, I had some of my street buddies over alongside a few family members. We were in the front room drinking Wild Turkey and beer shots. So, you know boys will be boys. I went into my room and brought out my Smith and Wesson mark three pistol. I loaded one round in the chamber, spun the barrel, put it up to the side of my head, and pulled the trigger. To my surprise, each one of my friends did the same thing. I said to them, let's see what you got, so I loaded two bullets inside, spun the barrel, stuck it to my head, and pulled the trigger. When I put it down to pass it around, my friend Frank said, you win, Bruce. He told me I wouldn't stop until somebody shot himself. My mother found out what I was doing and didn't talk to me for three months. All she said to me was you are crazy, and I told her I was not crazy; I just did not care.

I quickly found work with new employers, giving quotes for auto repair jobs to insurance companies. One day, a customer took me to lunch and asked me what I used to do and what I was planning to do with my life. I told him about my time in the war, and he ended up running a check on me to see who I was. He discovered I was familiar with explosives and many other weapons. He then asked me if I wanted to work for him and his friends. When I asked him what they did, he said they collected money from clients. When I asked him what my job included, he said, "You will be our bodyguard, drive the car, and live with us. He told me whatever we were into and we got caught, they would get me out; just don't tell anybody about us. So, I told him "not a problem." I also told him if he harmed anybody in my family and failed to kill me, I would hunt them down and kill everybody. You know what he said to me, "Right answer, we heard you have gold balls."

One time, we went to Reno, Nevada, to see some of his friends. It looked like a regular house in a typical neighborhood. We went into the garage, and the guy hit a button on the door. There was an elevator. We went down one story to come to another room. Inside, the room was full of weapons, C-4, and all kinds of other explosives. They had all the things that a ninja would have and even made their own gun silencers. All my boss told me was not to talk to anybody wherever we went. I asked him why, and he said they don't know who you are, and it intimidates them.

We went out in the desert, and they had high-tech military weapons. They put little targets in about 300 meters. All of the guys tried to hit the target, but they missed. So, my boss threw me the rifle and said knock them down. I hit all six targets in the sand, and his customers just looked at me and said who's this guy. That's why he didn't want me to talk to anybody.

One day, we were driving down the freeway, and somebody said, "See the red Maxima, catch up to him, and pull him over." One guy jumped out of the back, pulled a gun on him, and brought him to ride with us. They made a call to this guy's brother and told him you have one hour to pay us the $75,000 you owe us, or your brother is dead. They handed the phone to the brother. These guys aren't nobody to screw with. These guys had 15 different licenses, but nobody knew who they actually were.

I stayed with these guys for about two years, and they had something big that was going to open. They got new identities and passports. My cut would have been one million dollars. When we were ready to go, something went wrong. We all scattered, and they said they would be in touch with me, but I never heard from them again. So, I went back to the car business to work.

Twenty-Two

Bingo

I started to get my life back on track and secured a job working for Century Automotive. My mother loved bingo, and she would go to play at the local Samoan church. I was also a member of the Veterans of Foreign Wars in Santa Clara, and one of the members invited me out to their bingo, Tafatolu Church Bingo in Santa Clara. So I went a few times, and after maybe the fourth time going, I noticed a girl selling cherry bells (pull tabs) to help raise funds for the church dance. She told me they were having the dance next week and I should come support and have fun. She then asked me to come, but I turned her down initially because I didn't have anyone to go with me. So, I asked her to go, and she agreed!

I found out her name was Vau and waited about a week for her to call, but nothing. So that Sunday, I drove to find the church she mentioned and saw they were doing a choir practice, which they called "Pese" (music) practice. Her niece saw me outside, recognized me from that bingo night, went into their music practice, and said, "Hey, aunty! Your little friend is outside looking for you".

When she came out, she asked what I was doing there. I asked her, "What happened? They canceled the dance?" and she said, "No." So I drove her home that day just to spend a little time with her. She asked me to come inside and meet her family. Everyone was giving me a funny stare, wondering if I was her new "friend." She asked me to come back for lunch the following Sunday, and when I did, I was surprised to walk in and see everyone sitting on the floor with their legs folded. I immediately felt out of place because I knew I couldn't sit like that after getting shot in both of my knees in Nam. However, I managed and was introduced to her daughter.

After that, I stopped by almost every day after work to see them both. Her mother was Samoan and didn't talk in English too much. After I had known the family for a while, all the sisters used to ask me what my intentions were. I told them I didn't have to answer them, only to her mother. One day, Vau and I were watching TV on the couch, and her mother started yelling at her. I thought I did something wrong, but Vau said, "Wow, I'm surprised," and told me what her mother said. She told me to tell you to go get your clothes and move in with us. I was also surprised, but I took them up on the offer. Out of all the brothers and sisters, she was the only one who was not married yet. So, I think her mom said maybe there's somebody for her child to marry, which probably made her happy.

Another Samoan church dance came about, and we went. We had a great time. Vau drank a lot even though she wasn't a drinker like that. We got home; she was drunk, and I was feeling froggy. Vau warned me that her mother was still asleep, and I told her it was fine; boys will be boys. Before you know it, she was pregnant. I had to make sure I wasn't married to my ex-wife. By the time I got that out of the way, we then went to Reno and got married. Nine months later, we were rushing Vau to the hospital because she was in labor and wasn't feeling well.

Twenty-Three

Hope

When we arrived at the hospital, they hooked her up to central lines to monitor the baby's heart rate, and the heart rate kept dropping. It was high and then dropped really low, so they had to rush a cesarean delivery. She requested her niece Litara to be in the delivery room with her while I waited outside. Shortly thereafter, our daughter Hope was born but struggled to breathe. They had to operate on her quickly to get an airway for her to breathe. We found out she swallowed a lot of meconium while inside her mother's womb. Due to the lack of oxygen while Hope was inside the womb and at birth, the doctors weren't sure if Hope would have any other complications in years to come or if she would make it out of the operation as a newborn. Hope had to spend three months in the hospital in an incubator until she was strong enough to breathe on her own and reached a healthy weight.

When she was one, we noticed Hope wasn't crawling like normal babies. She was doing more of an army crawl and dragging her body behind her. Vau and I were concerned, so we scheduled an appointment to find out what was going on. Her doctor ran some tests and told us Hope had Cerebral Palsy. Several years went by, and Hope still struggled to crawl and walk and cried all night. I felt so bad as her father that I found a Stanford Hospital doctor by the name of Dr. Gamble, who was able to take a look at Hope and ordered surgery to be done on her hamstrings, which had been causing her the pain at night. He advised us he would cut some of her tendons to release the tightness and allow her more flexibility. After this operation, we did notice she slept better, but her mobility still did not improve.

Shortly afterward, I started receiving my Social Security and was able to buy us tickets to fly to Samoa to visit Vau's village. Vau had a cousin named To'o who did massages on people with muscle damage. He tried everything he could think to help Hope, even a technique where he would bury her legs in the sand and massage her on the beach, but to no avail. To this day, my daughter has never taken a step. Later she had her hip bone repositioned to make her feet stay together, and then she had to get braces on both her feet. I used to take her to therapy every week. One day she told me that the other kids used to stare at her. I told her they were just looking, but they didn't mean any harm.

While she was growing up, she kept asking me when would she be able to walk and get out of her wheelchair. As she got older, I explained to her that was the way she would probably be. I also told her there are a lot of kids that are way worse than her. You can feed yourself, and you are smart as a whip, you just probably will never walk. She said okay, Dad. Her mother was always there for her too. I knew when I saw the strength and resilience in Vau that I finally married the right woman. She had the best heart out of all anyone I knew.

Twenty-Four

House Fire

At this point, we were living our 13th year with my good friend John Kizzia, who moved to Oregon and let us stay in his home because it was easier for our daughter to get in and out and around the house in her wheelchair. Hope graduated high school in 2013 and was on her 2nd full semester of Junior College at DeAnza when Vau and I flew to Hawaii to visit her brother for his birthday. On the second day, we got a phone call that our house was on fire. Our immediate thought was of Hope. We were so relieved to hear she was in school and no one was home but Vau's nieces, who were helping with Hope while we were away. They were safe and able to get out. The worst part is that we lived right across the street from the Fire Department. The Red Cross gave them money for food and whatever else they needed until I got home. By the time we got back from Hawaii and returned to the house, the Firemen said we couldn't go inside because everything we owned had been destroyed.

Some people would have given up, but not me because I'm a soldier. I could sleep in my car, but not them. Thank goodness I had insurance for incidents like this, and we were fortunate enough to stay at the Marriot for almost nine months for free. Once that ended, friends from the Bingo Hall told us to move in with them until we got on our feet again. He only had one small room available, but it was better than nothing. We had no luck finding a home during the whole time in the hotel, and I had to file bankruptcy because I was still paying for some of the stuff we lost. The Veteran's Affairs office made us wait two years, but I was finally able to finally get approved for a home loan of $350,000.

Finding a home in the Bay Area for the three of us proved seemingly impossible. We looked all over Silicon Valley, East Bay, South Bay, and North Bay. We finally found a home in the Valley area called Los Banos. The house was barely a year old and would only cost $320,000. This was perfect so far, but Vau didn't want to leave Silicon Valley because of Hope's doctors. Finding no other alternative, we took the house, and when we finally moved in, my wife and daughter loved our home.

Twenty-Five

The Stroke

I had an annual check-up with my primary doctor, who advised me after all my tests that if I wanted to stick around to care for Hope, I better quit drinking. The next day, I did and remained sober for over 25 years. The first week of February 2019, we went to Circus Circus in Reno for my birthday. One night, my wife came into the room, and I was sitting crooked in bed and could not speak. She hollered to our niece Danette, who was with us on the trip with her daughter Eva and Hope. Danette came running to see what happened and saw Vau struggling to sit me up. Danette hurried over, tried getting my attention, and called 911. Vau ran to get a wet towel and slapped me in the face with it to help me come to, but I was still not all there.

Before you know it, an ambulance was there, and I was being taken out on a stretcher. Anyone who knows me knows I am not weak, and being wheeled out of my favorite casino was not my finest hour. I went three minutes across the street to Saint Mary's Hospital, where the doctors said I had suffered a double stroke.

The doctors told Vau they needed to inject me with a drug that could very much save my life or cause me to die in hours. Vau felt so much pressure because she wasn't sure about anything with this drug, but she had an hour to make a decision. She decided to have them inject me because she did not want to do nothing, and something happened in the worst way. So she took a chance, and it worked.

I was hospitalized for three days. The Circus Circus casino we stayed at was so kind to credit our rooms for the extra four days because Vau and I had been loyal players for many years, and they wanted to make sure I was taken care of. The day I was discharged was a miraculous moment for the hospital staff that cared for me because they saw me get out of bed on my own and walk back to the casino with Danette. They said there was no way anyone should be able to walk away from a double stroke, but my wife did the right thing because she knew I was a fighter and I always make it out. Vau told the hospital, "You guys don't know my husband. He's tough," sure enough, they saw that. My brain was coming back to me, and my speech was a little blurred, but one side of my body was okay. I figured Jesus wasn't ready for me.

Twenty-Six

Reunions and Goodbyes

Shortly after the fateful Reno trip, we planned another one for my 70th birthday. Vau, being the worry bee she was because of my stroke, wanted me to have a lovely birthday that I would definitely remember. She got in touch with my three daughters from my previous marriages, Serena, Sharee, and Shannon, on Facebook and invited them to my birthday trip to Reno. I tell you, I was so surprised when I saw them in the lobby of Circus Circus. I immediately recognized them all. Vau and Hope kept it a secret from me this whole time and even paid for their tickets to fly out to be with me in Reno. I was still in such shock because I had not seen my three girls for over 15 years. I said, "I know you guys probably hate me," but all they said was they knew their mother and I had problems; you can't fool children. I told them how I never called them up because I felt guilty about walking out on them, but there wasn't a day that went by that I didn't think about them. Now, we talk regularly, and I have even been able to go out to North Carolina to spend time with them and meet my grandchildren. If it had not been for Vau, I never would have had this second chance to be close to my girls again.

A month or so later, Vau got a call from her village in Samoa that the high chief had passed away, and it was customary for her to return home for the funeral. She was there for a couple of weeks, and when she returned, she had a cough that she couldn't get rid of. Danette would visit us often and took Vau to the emergency room just to be safe. While there, they told her they noticed a large mass that could highly be pneumonia or something serious. So they prescribed antibiotics for the pneumonia and said if it did not relieve any pain, then we should seriously consider looking into seeing a Lung Cancer specialist.

It took many failed appointments and a distressing lack of communication from these doctor offices before we were able to schedule a visit to the Cancer Center in Merced, where they would finally do a complete evaluation to determine if she had cancer. The staff there panicked when they heard her breathing and called for the ambulance to come get her. Everyone was already on edge due to COVID-19, and I think they didn't want to take a chance and treat her even though they noticed her breathing was better with the oxygen tank.

Unfortunately, the next morning, we got a call that my wife had passed. She coded three times when they tried to intubate her. That was the saddest and hardest day of my life. Something about the way she woke up the day before her appointment just didn't seem right, but I didn't say much. I had no idea that was going to be the last time I saw her. I did not cry when my mother passed, but I cried when I lost my wife. I cried when I had to tell our daughter that she passed. Vau used to always joke about me missing her if she was ever to go before me, and I would rudely reply back, "Nope, not a chance." But she was right. I miss her so much every day. I would give anything to have her back.

Danette and her daughter Eva moved in with us permanently, and shortly after, so did Litara, Danette's mother. Having them here with me takes the weight off my shoulders of worrying about Hope. I have a piece of Vau here who is still helping me care for my daughter, and because of that, I know I will never have to worry about it. Hope truly is in the best hands.

Twenty-Seven

Epilogue

If I had to give any advice to people who get depressed, just hang in there. There's a lot of people out there to help you. Do not turn to drugs or booze because it never works. Just suck it up and keep going. It has been many years since the Vietnam War, and I still can't sleep more than two to three hours without waking up. I thought that all of the drinking I did helped me sleep, but in the long run, it just made me sick with liver and other problems.

At one time in my life, I was into money, fast cars, jewelry, and material things. When you really get sick, or something happens to you, the only thing you have left is your family. Of all my brothers and sisters, I had the hardest time showing emotion because I believed soldiers are supposed to be that way.

I think Jesus put us all down here to see what we are made of. So, if you're a Christian and believe in the Bible about Adam and Eve, then all of us on this planet are related. If I look back on my life, I think I did so much of what I did because of guilt. I saw so many guys that came home like me with nobody to talk to because of the war. I used to do some drugs, but little stuff. As far as drinking, I just never stopped. I wasn't afraid of anybody or anything. Sometimes, my mother would say, "Are you trying to kill yourself?" and she was probably right. I look at the soldiers returning from the Middle East and see why some end up in jail or committing suicide. It seems like many of our citizens only like soldiers if we all do our duty to keep them free. All of the soldiers that went to any war are pretty much the same. We soldiers stick together because nobody can take that away from us.

AMEN Bruce Smith

Bruce Smith is a Vietnam War veteran who served three tours of duty. He returned to the United States and became a valued member of his community while overcoming the effects of PTSD. This is his story.

Printed in the USA
CPSIA information can be obtained
at www.ICGtesting.com
LVHW080252280124
769814LV00005B/120